July 2017

D0113254

HONEST ABE — LITTLE WHITE LIE — BIG OL' WHOPPER

NATIONAL GEOGRAPHIC KiDS

REAL

OR

FAKE? 2

MORE
FAR-OUT FIBS, FISHY FACTS, AND PHONY PHOTOS TO TEST FOR THE TRUTH

EMILY KRIEGER
ILLUSTRATIONS BY TOM NICK COCOTOS

NATIONAL GEOGRAPHIC
WASHINGTON, D.C.

CONTENTS

Welcome to
REAL OR FAKE...

... the book that **TESTS YOUR INNER LIE DETECTOR!** Before you try to sort fact from fib, let's go over these few tips:

How do you identify a lie? Sometimes it's hard to put your finger on a fake, but here are a few clues to help you along the way:

DETAILS, DETAILS, DETAILS

Be on the lookout for details in a story that are inconsistent, or just seem impossible. Also, people have a tendency to over-explain when they're feeling guilty about something; likewise, some details in these stories just aren't necessary. Sometimes that can be a key identifier in figuring out where the truth is stretched.

IF SOMETHING SEEMS FISHY ...

... it probably is! Experience is one of the best teachers in life, so use yours when trying to determine what is real and what is fake.

GO WITH YOUR GUT

If things seem too unbelievable to be true, oftentimes they are. Trust your instincts when things seem off—a good rule for this book and in life!

LITTLE WHITE LIE

HONEST ABE

BIG OL' WHOPPER

WHAT'S A FIB-O-METER? A fib-o-meter is a handy little gauge we've invented for determining the level of a lie (or truth). The categories are: Honest Abe, Little White Lie, and Big Ol' Whopper. We've gone through and determined which story falls where based on whether it's true or how big a lie it is. If the story is true it falls in Honest Abe territory. If the details of the story are untrue and the lie is minor, we've gone with Little White Lie. If it was a big lie that maybe led to something else (widespread panic or disbelief, maybe), we've gone with Big Ol' Whopper. Agree with our findings? Decide for yourself as you rate things on the fib-o-meter!

AUSTRALIA ORDERS
CATS INDOORS

Pity Australia's house cats. The government is asking that they please not go outdoors. Ever. It may seem crazy, but the country has a good reason for keeping kitties inside: They're killers. When let loose, the seemingly sweet, purring pets pounce on Australia's native animals and eat them up. So much so that some of the small mammal and bird species preyed upon by cats are now perilously close to extinction. These species lived without cats until a few hundred years ago, when European settlers brought them down under. Since then, the cats have exploded in number while the native critter numbers have dwindled. So the solution, says Australia's threatened species commissioner, is extreme: Keep cats indoors! Perhaps even worse for the cats: The curfew doesn't apply to dogs!

9

REAL

HONEST ABE

AUSTRALIA'S THREATENED SPECIES COMMISSIONER CAUSED A COMMOTION IN 2015 WHEN HE ANNOUNCED ALL CATS SHOULD BE KEPT INSIDE. For now, the 24-hour cat containment is only a request and not a law. Some parts of Australia, though, do have a rule requiring any cat that goes outside be kept contained or on a leash.

FUN FACT

In the 1800s, the Australian government released cats into the wild to CONTROL NON-NATIVE RABBITS AND HOUSE MICE.

BEAVERS PARACHUTE
INTO IDAHO

REAL OR FAKE?

Look up in the sky! It's a bird! It's a plane! It's a … beaver? Believe it or not, back in the mid-1900s, a bunch of beavers parachuted into a forest in central Idaho, U.S.A. These rodents weren't daredevils. Rather, wildlife authorities sent the beavers skydiving because they were causing problems in their original homes elsewhere in the state. The authorities wanted to send the animals to a remote wilderness area. But getting there by foot or car proved problematic. So someone suggested parachuting the animals in. Pairs of beavers of equal size and weight were put in wooden boxes with holes drilled into them. Then the boxes were wound with rope in a way that ensured they would easily open upon landing. Last but not least, parachutes were attached to the boxes. Each flight dropped 10 boxes, or 20 beavers, into the wilderness area. Amazingly, they landed safely!

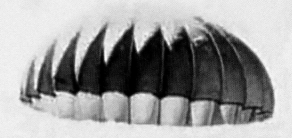

The AMERICAN BEAVER, at about 40 pounds (18 kg), is the largest rodent in North America. But more than a million years ago, the aptly named giant beaver was even bigger: It weighed up to 220 pounds (100 kg) and was 8 feet (2.5 m) long!

REAL

HONEST ABE

THIS IS ONE CRAZY IDEA THAT WORKED.

It made the news first in 1950 and again in 2015, when someone found a long-lost film of a beaver airdrop. The footage shows the furry critters falling from the sky and scurrying out of their boxes into mountain meadows. Beavers are still relocated in the state, but an Idaho wildlife official says they haven't used the parachute practice in 50 years.

SCHOOL REPLACES
STAIRS WITH SLIDES

REAL OR FAKE?

A New York City school went from average to supercool in 2014 when it replaced all of its stairs with something way better—slides! Twenty-two bright-yellow plastic slides were installed in place of stairs at Northeast Elementary. Since then the school's 500-plus students not only have more fun getting around, they also get to where they're going quicker. The principal came up with the idea after noticing how long it took kids to travel between the building's floors and that the stairs were a tripping hazard for younger students. Parents of the students were invited to school to look at sketches of the slides and then vote on whether to install them. The slides-instead-of-stairs idea won by a landslide, and the following summer the plan was put into action. The change was a hit with students, and teachers are pleased, too: Tardiness has decreased 49 percent!

CAFETERIA →

The world's longest inflatable water slide is 1,975 feet (601.98 m) long and takes MORE THAN A MINUTE TO TRAVEL FROM TOP TO BOTTOM.

A SCHOOL WITH ONLY SLIDES AND NO STAIRS WOULD BE AWESOME BUT IMPRACTICAL:

How would people get to upper floors if every single stair were removed? There is, however, a university that installed slides for its students. The Technical University of Munich, in Germany, has two enclosed, four-story slides in one of its buildings. But students still have to use stairs to travel to the upper floors.

IDENTIFY THE LIE!

For each question group below, two statements are TRUE, and one is FALSE. Can you put your finger on the fib?

1

A. The oldest fossilized human poop is 5,000 years old.

B. A study found that when given a choice, chimps prefer their food cooked instead of raw.

C. When asked to name a new polar research vessel in 2016, the British public overwhelmingly picked *Boaty McBoatface*.

2

A. The World Toe Wrestling Championship is held annually in England.

B. A chicken McNugget shaped like George Washington sold for $8,100 in 2012.

C. Scientists made cheese from bacteria found behind grizzly bear ears.

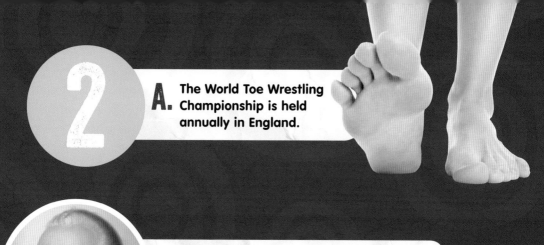

ANSWERS: 1. A: Fake! The oldest preserved piece of poop from a human was unearthed in Spain and is actually far older—about 50,000 years old! Analyses of the poop revealed its owner was omnivorous, or ate both plants and animals. 2. C: Fake! The truth is even worse: Scientists made cheese from bacteria found in people's belly buttons and mouths and the spaces between their toes! Each cheese is supposed to smell like the person the bacteria came from. Ew!

21

WHERE PEOPLE IRON
THEIR UNDERWEAR

Why would anyone iron their underwear? In sub-Saharan Africa, people have a good reason. They steam their skivvies to make sure maggots—fly larvae—don't end up living inside their skin! Female flies like to lay their eggs on damp clothes and linens drying on a laundry line. Unless you have a dryer, which many people in the region don't, you can't stop them from doing this. But you can kill the eggs—by ironing. So people iron everything from towels to trousers to underwear. It takes time and may seem silly, but it's worth it: If it is not destroyed, an egg hatches and lets loose a larva (a maggot) that burrows into your skin. There it feasts on your tissue for a while before squeezing out of your skin through a painful bump!

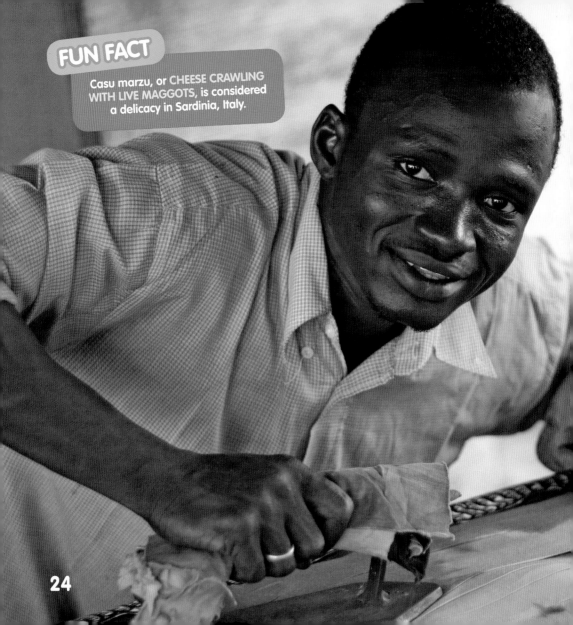

24

REAL

HONEST
ABE

IN AFRICAN COUNTRIES SOUTH OF THE SAHARA, IT'S NOT UNCOMMON TO SEE PEOPLE IRONING THEIR UNDERWEAR.

They fear the insect that goes by several names: the tumbu fly, the putzi fly, or the mango fly. By the time it wriggles out of you, it's an alarming size: 0.5 to 0.6 inches (1.3-1.5 cm) long!

STORE'S
INSANE DEALS

Black Friday, the day following Thanksgiving, has become a major shopping event in America. Stores open as early as midnight, lines of shoppers stretch for blocks outside, and once inside, people fight over everything, even toys! The competition among stores to attract customers is fierce, so in 2015 a popular retail chain store offered deals that no one else could. But the deals were so weird that customers were left wondering whether they even wanted them! Flyers found in stores and online advertised oddities such as a free falcon (with a purchase of $75 or more), enchanted mayonnaise (only $1.99!), a Skittles flat-screen TV (since when did the candy brand start making electronics?), and an invitation to Kyle's bar mitzvah ($59.99, which included dancing, a DJ, face painting, and food). Though a lot of businesses advertise "insane" deals, these deals really were crazy!

BATTERY CENTER

FUN FACT

The same comedian has pulled several in-store pranks, including posting fake, silly product reviews alongside items for sale in another popular retail store. A REVIEW HE PLACED ON A RUG READ: "WORST MAGIC CARPET EVER."

LITTLE WHITE LIE

FAKE!

THE WACKY ADS WERE THE WORK OF A CALIFORNIA, U.S.A.-BASED COMEDIAN, WHO POSTED THEM AT A STORE NEAR HIS HOME AND ON ONE OF HIS SOCIAL MEDIA ACCOUNTS.

He wanted to poke fun at the ridiculous lengths people and stores go to for Black Friday. Other deals in the pages-long fake ad included a fanny pack filled with pudding for $9.99 and a tent with an angry opossum in it for $24.99!

DANCING
GOES TO THE DOGS

REAL OR FAKE?

You've likely seen dancing competitions on TV... but have you heard of dog dancing competitions? You may imagine two canines cutting a rug. But in reality, at these competitions a dog and its human handler perform a choreographed dance! Participants around the world use costumes, props, and songs to create performances with themes that range from Roman gladiators to the Wild West. The sport held its first worldwide competition in 2000, and divisions include "Sassy Seniors," for older dogs and people, and "Handi-Dandi Dancers," for "creatively challenged" performers. Participants are judged on both their artistry and technicality, and can have points deducted for everything from missing a step in the routine to excessive talking and barking. Dogs that poop or pee during their routine are automatically disqualified. That's ruff!

REAL

HONEST ABE

BELIEVE IT OR NOT, DOG DANCING IS REAL.
Called canine freestyle, the sport first emerged in the 1980s and competitions are held throughout the year by the World Canine Freestyle Organization. Its founder, a former ballroom dancer (and human), has high hopes for the sport: She hopes to one day see it in the Olympics! With more than 30 chapters worldwide, it certainly seems possible!

SCIENTISTS SEND
MESSAGE TO ALIENS

REAL OR FAKE?

Do you like fun facts? Scientists hope aliens do. Hurtling through space, way past Pluto, is a disk that holds hundreds of fun facts about Earth. Launched by NASA in 1977, the disk includes everything from images of chimps and people to the sounds of surf and Beethoven's Fifth Symphony. Like a buried time capsule, it contains a message for whoever finds it—in this case, aliens, scientists hope. Called the Golden Record, it bears spoken greetings in 55 languages and is intended to educate otherworldly beings about Earth and its inhabitants. The information on the 12-inch (30-cm) gold-plated copper disk was compiled by a team of scientists led by famous astronomer Carl Sagan. Just imagine: One day an alien in a solar system far, far away could be looking at photos of animals while listening to classical music. Far out!

REAL

NOT ONE BUT TWO OF THESE DISKS WERE SENT INTO SPACE IN 1977 ABOARD THE IDENTICAL VOYAGER 1 AND 2 SPACECRAFT.

The craft are traveling on different paths and beam back scientific information about their surroundings to Earth. Now in interstellar space—the space between our star, the sun, and other stars—Voyager 1 is the most distant human-made object in space.

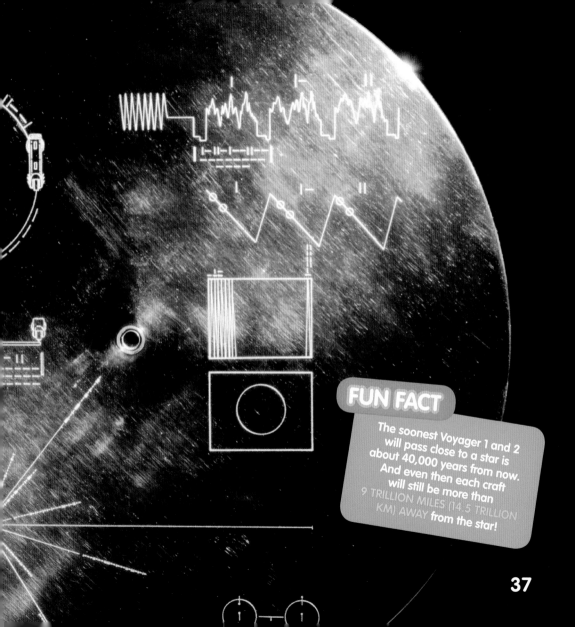

GREETINGS FROM OUTER SPACE!

Can you guess which greetings are ABOARD THE GOLDEN RECORD and which are MADE UP?

1 "Greetings to our friends in the stars. We wish that we will meet you someday." (Arabic)

2 "Peace" (Hebrew)

3 "Good night, ladies and gentlemen. Goodbye and see you next time." (Indonesian)

4 "Yo!" (French)

5 "Hello from the children of planet Earth." (English)

6 "Hope everyone's well. We are thinking about you all. Please come here to visit when you have time." (Mandarin Chinese)

7 "Greetings, alien life-forms. We ask that you please not blow up or take over planet Earth."
(Dutch)

8 "We greet you, O great ones."
(Sotho)

9 "How are all you people of other planets?"
(Nyanja)

10 "Greetings from a human being of the Earth. Please contact."
(Gujarati)

11 "Greetings from a computer programmer in the little university town of Ithaca on the planet Earth."
(Swedish)

12 "Hello? Anybody out there?"
(Spanish)

13 "Friends of space, how are you all? Have you eaten yet? Come visit us if you have time."
(Amoy)

Answers: 1. Real; 2. Real; 3. Real; 4. Real; 5. Real; 6. Real; 7. Fake; 8. Real; 9. Real; 10. Real; 11. Real; 12. Real; 13. Real.

15-FOOT PENGUIN
WADDLES ASHORE

REAL OR FAKE?

Everyone agrees penguins are adorable. But what if one stood 15 feet (4.5 m) tall? Would it still be cute? Scary? Floridians found themselves pondering just such a penguin in 1948, when three-toed footprints each about a foot (0.3 m) across and long were found along the shore of the Gulf of Mexico in the small seaside city of Clearwater, Florida, U.S.A. Experts who investigated the imprints in the sand said that whatever made them must weigh nearly 2,000 pounds (907 kg). And it wasn't a sea turtle. So what was it? Additional investigations pointed to a previously unknown species of penguin that would tower over people. Visitors flocked to the town to be the first to spot the creature, now called the Florida Giant Penguin or the Clearwater Monster. The tracks kept turning up, sometimes on other beaches, until 1958. To this day scientists have never seen the big bird.

FAKE!

THE FLORIDA GIANT PENGUIN WAS A HOAX, OR TRICK, INSPIRED BY PHOTOGRAPHS OF FOSSILIZED DINOSAUR FOOTPRINTS IN *NATIONAL GEOGRAPHIC*. A Clearwater man named Tony Signorini crafted metal three-toed feet with his co-worker, a known prankster, and stomped around in the sand while wearing them to make the footprints. The jokers kept their secret until 1988, when Signorini spilled the beans.

THE WHITE HOUSE'S
CHEESY HISTORY

REAL OR FAKE?

Did you know that several presidents have invited people to the White House...to eat cheese? It started in 1801, when a four-foot (1.2-m)-wide, 1,235-pound (560-kg) wheel of cheese arrived after a three-week sleigh and ship ride from Cheshire, Massachusetts, U.S.A. The town's citizens had sent it to celebrate Thomas Jefferson's presidential victory. To get rid of it (and score some points with voters), he invited Americans into his house on New Year's Day to whittle away at the wheel. In 1835, President Andrew Jackson received a 1,400-pound (635-kg) cheddar. Two years later, on George Washington's birthday, Jackson opened his home to thousands of hungry Americans. They took only two hours to polish off the cheese (which had reportedly started to stink). In 1928, President Calvin Coolidge was gifted a 147-pound (67-kg) Swiss. The son of a cheesemaker and big fan of the food, he shared it only with his Secret Service.

REAL

HONEST
ABE

THERE'S MORE THAN ONE TYPE OF "BIG CHEESE" IN THE WHITE HOUSE! In honor of this wacky tradition, the White House began Big Block of Cheese Day in 2014. Sadly, there's no sharing of cheese on this day. Instead, the White House shares its time and information, answering questions from people on social media for an entire day in January.

ALASKA'S
WACKY GEOGRAPHY

REAL OR FAKE?

Did you know the easternmost and westernmost points in the United States are both in Alaska? It may sound crazy, but the reason it's true could sound even crazier: It's because of an invisible line dividing Earth into two halves. This line encircles Earth from top to bottom, passing through both poles and the Atlantic and Pacific Oceans. Where it passes through the Atlantic Ocean, everything east of it is the Eastern Hemisphere, while everything west of it is the Western Hemisphere. On the other side of Earth, where this line passes through the Pacific, a chain of Alaskan islands straddles it. In the Western Hemisphere, Amatignak Island is closest to the line. A mere 63 miles (101 km) away, on the other side of the line, in the Eastern Hemisphere, sits Semisopochnoi Island—the easternmost point in the United States. What a big difference a little distance can make!

REAL

HONEST
ABE

THIS LINE IS JUST ONE OF MANY ENCIRCLING EARTH THAT GEOGRAPHERS CALL LONGITUDE AND LATITUDE. Lines of longitude are vertical and pass through the poles. Lines of latitude are horizontal; the Equator, which encircles the middle of the globe like a belt, is a line of latitude. Though imaginary, the lines are treated as if they're real, to help keep order on Earth. Before people agreed on the lines' locations, more than a century ago, maps varied from country to country.

PECULIAR PLACE-NAMES

Study any map and you'll know that some place-names sound funnier than others, but are these too unbelievable to be TRUE? Some of them are! Can you figure out WHICH ONES?

1 PITY ME, ENGLAND, UNITED KINGDOM

2 PEA SOUP, SWAZILAND

3 BABY, POLAND

4 DRAGON'S BREATH, NEW ZEALAND

5 PUNKEYDOODLES CORNERS, ONTARIO, CANADA

6 NO NAME, COLORADO, U.S.A.

7 HUMANSVILLE, MISSOURI, U.S.A.

8 ANGRY BIRD, THAILAND

9 SAINT-LOUIS-DU-HA! HA!, QUEBEC, CANADA

10 ITTY-BITTY, PERU

11 UGLEY, ENGLAND, UNITED KINGDOM

ANSWERS: 1. Real; 2. Fake; 3. Real; 4. Fake; 5. Real; 6. Real; 7. Real; 8. Fake; 9. Real; 10. Fake; 11. Real

MAN SNEEZES OUT 44-YEAR-OLD TOY

REAL OR FAKE?

Imagine this: A British man sneezed out a toy part that had been stuck in his head for 44 years! It may sound like sweet relief. But the man never even knew the part had been inside him! After experiencing a sneezing fit and "a very uncomfortable sensation," he felt something plugging up his left nostril and plucked it out. To his surprise, it was a small rubber suction cup. Curious, he called his mother to tell her about the weird incident. She recalled she had thought he had swallowed the sucker, part of a toy dart, when he was about seven years old. Worried, she had taken him to the hospital and had him examined, but nothing was found. The man says his nose doesn't feel any different than before and that he never had trouble blowing his nose or smelling. Amazingly, the stuck toy seems to have remained harmless over all those decades.

REAL

HONEST
ABE

FUN FACT

In 2013, a Brazilian family found their
PET TORTOISE—alive—after it had been
MISSING FOR MORE THAN 30 YEARS!
They had assumed it had run (walked
slowly?) away in 1982 but it had really
been locked in a storage room since then.

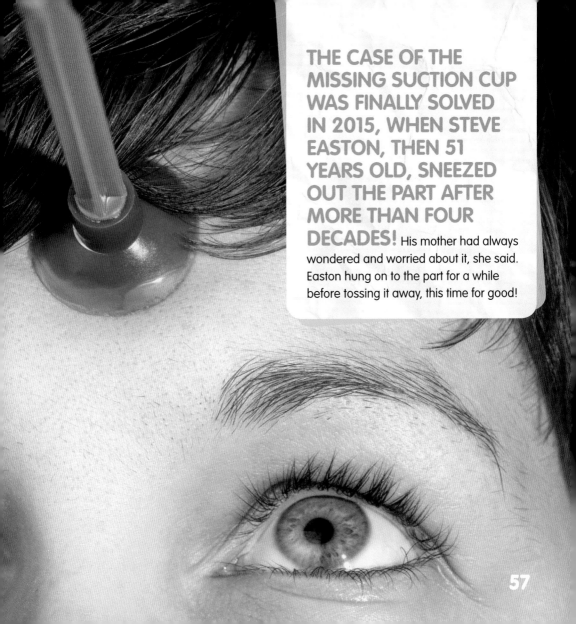

THE CASE OF THE MISSING SUCTION CUP WAS FINALLY SOLVED IN 2015, WHEN STEVE EASTON, THEN 51 YEARS OLD, SNEEZED OUT THE PART AFTER MORE THAN FOUR DECADES! His mother had always wondered and worried about it, she said. Easton hung on to the part for a while before tossing it away, this time for good!

57

WACKY HEADLINES

Extra! Extra! Read all about it! Some of the headlines below are totally made up, but some have actually been published. Read on to see if you can determine which are the FAKES.

1 WOMAN BUILDS TWO-STORY HOUSE FOR HER PET PIGEON

2 CANADIAN LAKE FALLS OFF CLIFF

3 GAME SHOW CONTESTANT LETS CAT PICK CORRECT ANSWER, WINS $1,000,000

4 MAN NAMED BACON ARRESTED FOR FIGHT OVER SAUSAGE

5 ZOO'S ESCAPED ELECTRIC EEL KNOCKS OUT POWER ACROSS ENGLAND

6 'ALIEN' SIGNAL FROM SPACE WAS A GUY REHEATING PIZZA

7 PILOT'S ARM FALLS OFF WHILE LANDING PLANE

8 GIANT INFLATABLE RED BALL TERRORIZES CITY OF TOLEDO

9 TEEN RIDES BIKE 13 MILES TO SCHOOL IN HIS SLEEP

10 COW URINE MAKES FOR JUICY LEMONS

11 TWO DOGS TAKE OWNER'S TRUCK FOR A JOYRIDE

12 COLLEGE STUDENT 3D PRINTS HIS OWN BRACES

ANSWERS: 1, 3, 5, and 9 are fake.

SHARKS BABBLE
WITH BUBBLES

REAL OR FAKE?

It may sound fishy, but sharks "talk" to each other by blowing bubbles, says a new study. Scientists studying great white sharks off the coast of South Africa report that the bubbles seen floating from the mouths of these fearsome fish actually mean something. The scientists watched 23 different great whites for more than 200 hours over several months, from the safety of an underwater cage. They recorded the number of bubbles and how much time passed between each bubble batch. After spending days studying the patterns, they figured out what a few meant. A massive amount of teeny-tiny bubbles every 20 seconds means "Food nearby!" A single bubble means "Danger!" And three bubbles released one after another means "Get lost, this is my territory!" With the help of a bubble machine, scientists were even able to join the conversation!

FUN FACT

Scientists are studying whether BURSTS OF BIG BUBBLES can be used to scare off great white sharks.

FAKE!

BIG OL' WHOPPER

IT WOULD BE COOL TO BE ABLE TO TALK TO FISH, BUT IT HASN'T HAPPENED. Scientists did, however, find out in 2003 that herring communicate with each other by releasing bubbles—from their rear ends! What's even funnier: It's the sound the bubbles make that's important. Herring listen to each other's toots to "talk"!

SQUIRREL
STALKS WOMAN

REAL OR FAKE?

The Bottrop, Germany, police department got its most unusual case yet when a woman called to complain that she was being stalked. Her description of the culprit at first didn't sound funny: reddish-brown hair, beady eyes, twitchy mouth. But then she added the creep also had whiskers and could fit in your hand. It was a squirrel, she said, and it had been following her. And she was starting to freak out. It sounded like a joke, but the police treated it as a real complaint, tracking down the suspicious squirrel, taking it into custody, and "searching" it at the station. They found the rodent wasn't nuts, just really tired. So they fed it honey and instead of sending it to the slammer, sent it to an animal rescue center for some rest and relaxation. Crazy case closed!

REAL

HONEST
ABE

THE STORY GOT WORLDWIDE ATTENTION IN 2015 WHEN THE POLICE DEPARTMENT POSTED A VIDEO TO SOCIAL MEDIA OF AN OFFICER FEEDING THE SQUIRREL. In the clip, which so far has racked up almost half a million views, the suspect looks much more adorable than menacing. Maybe the fur ball just wanted to be friends?

In 2015, when 28,000 pounds (12.7 t) of nuts went missing in Shelby Township, Michigan, U.S.A., police posted a plea for help from the public that included A MUG SHOT OF A SQUIRREL! It was a funny way to ask for help cracking the case, but the cost of the missing nuts was no laughing matter: $128,000.

WOMAN SEARCHES FOR HERSELF

Have you ever heard someone say, "I need to go find myself"? This means to do some soul-searching, or to figure out who you are. Except in one hilarious case out of Iceland: A woman ended up joining a search party in search of herself! Part of a bus tour group, she had exited and changed clothes at a stop and, upon reboarding, gone unrecognized by the bus driver. After an hour of waiting, the alarmed driver alerted authorities that a passenger had gone missing. About fifty people set out in search of the woman near the stop, a volcanic canyon more than 100 miles (161 km) east of the capital city, Reykjavík. The search was called off in the early hours of the next day when someone finally figured out that the missing person was, in fact, found, and had never even been lost.

FUN FACT

The volcanic canyon the woman was lost and found in, Eldgjá, is the largest in the world, plunging 885 FEET (270 M) DEEP AND STRETCHING 1,970 FEET (600 M) ACROSS.

REAL

HONEST
ABE

IN 2012, THIS SILLY SEARCH PARTY SET OUT AFTER THE DRIVER AND OTHER PASSENGERS FAILED TO RECOGNIZE THE WOMAN AND SHE FAILED TO RECOGNIZE THE DESCRIPTION OF THE MISSING PERSON AS HERSELF: "Asian, about 160 cm [5.3 feet], in dark clothing and speaks English well." The chief of police reported that the woman "had no idea that she was missing" and was not at fault.

SPOT THE FAKE!

Do you have the eye of a spy? See if you can tell which of these photos are REAL and which are really FAKE!

A praying mantis makes a great snake hat!

This juggling act is a real dog and pony show!

1

At a fair in Essex, England, pigs really did fly!

For a few seconds, this bird hitched a high-flying ride!

2

DOG TAKES BUS
BY ITSELF

REAL OR FAKE?

Talk about a ruff commute: A black Labrador in Seattle, Washington, U.S.A., named Eclipse has figured out how to take the bus by herself to the dog park! People started noticing the pooch seemed to be on the bus regularly without an owner. They didn't mind; by all accounts Eclipse is a friendly pup. Though she does sometimes pant in her seatmates' faces and has been known to lick the seats on the bus. It soon became clear that Eclipse had a routine: She got on the bus at the same stop and exited at another a short ways away—the dog park, naturally. Riders say she likes to be able to see out the window, so she knows when the bus arrives at her stop. The clever canine is just like the human riders—except she doesn't have to pay!

REAL

HONEST ABE

ECLIPSE'S OWNER SAYS SHE HOPPED ONTO THE BUS WITHOUT HIM ONE DAY WHEN HE WAS LOLLYGAGGING ON THE SIDEWALK. They'd taken the bus many times from their downtown home to the nearby park—apparently, so many times that Eclipse knew how to get there by heart! So her owner now lets her go to the park by herself when she feels like it. It's a win-win!

IDENTIFY THE LIE!

For each question group below, two statements are TRUE, and one is FALSE. Can you put your finger on the fib?

1

A. Women in Saudi Arabia weren't allowed to vote until 2015.

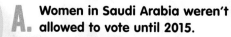

B. The record for most watermelons smashed with a head in 60 seconds is 27.

C. *Petrichor* is the word for the smell of rain hitting the earth.

80

2

A. Hungry bats in search of food listen for the sound of other bats snacking.

B. The carpet at the Portland International Airport, in Oregon, U.S.A., has its own social media account.

C. Most kangaroos are right-handed.

ANSWERS: 1. B: Fake! The record is actually 47 melons in a minute—talk about really using your head! John Allwood, a melon picker from Australia, performed the feat in 2009. 2. C: Fake! Most kangaroos are actually left-handed, a 2015 study found. Scientists report that red kangaroos and eastern gray kangaroos usually use their left paws. The finding was funny but also a big deal—previously, scientists had thought only humans had a hand preference.

THE DIRT ON
CHOCOLATE

REAL OR FAKE?

Nearly everyone loves chocolate. But did you know the popular sweet has a dirty little secret? While most people know it's made from cocoa beans, there's another key ingredient that's largely kept under wraps: dirt. That's right, mixed into every bite of chocolate is a little bit of dirt. It sounds icky, but chefs say dirt is essential to the dessert's flavor. For example, chocolate made with dirt from Madagascar tastes nuttier, while chocolate made with dirt from Venezuela tastes tangier. What makes one scoop of dirt different from another? More than just rock dust, dirt also contains bits of debris from rotten, once-living things like leaves and insects. So a region's plants and animals help shape the flavor of chocolate produced there. Perhaps this ingredient is a perfect example of ignorance is bliss?

secret
ingredient

People in the American South eat a type of clay called **WHITE DIRT.**

FAKE!

BIG OL' WHOPPER

CHOCOLATE IS MADE FROM COCOA BEANS, BUT NOT DIRT.
People do intentionally eat dirt, though. The practice is called geophagy, and the desire to eat dirt can be intense, especially among pregnant women. Scientists aren't sure why, but they do know people have been eating dirt for thousands of years. Still, not all dirt is safe to eat and you run the risk of ingesting harmful materials along with it. Do not try this at home!

COW MAKES
SPECIAL MILK

A **dairy farmer in Wisconsin, U.S.A.,** owns one sweet cow: It makes chocolate- and strawberry-flavored milk! Sam Stone says he feeds the cow, named Bessie, a typical diet of grains but that she's had a sneaky way of supplementing her meals since she was a calf. Bessie sometimes wanders into the family kitchen and eats whatever she finds. Stone is a champion pie-baker and often has piles of chocolate and strawberries on the table. So Bessie has developed quite a taste for the two treats. When she was old enough to be milked, Stone was shocked to discover that one udder squirted milk with a chocolate flavor, while the other one squirted milk with a slight strawberry flavor. And, yes, the chocolate milk is a light brown color, and the strawberry milk a pale pink. Stone says he no longer has to hassle his kids about milking Bessie: "They fight over who gets to do it!"

FAKE!

LITTLE WHITE LIE

SORRY, THERE'S NO SUCH THING AS A COW THAT MAKES MULTIPLE FLAVORS OF MILK.

The chocolate and strawberry flavors are added to regular milk; they don't come straight from the cow. There is, however, a freaky tree that grows 40 types of fruit. An artist created it by binding branches from different types of trees to a single tree. In the spring it bears many-colored blossoms, and in the summer its branches droop with all kinds of fruit!

FUN FACT

A dairy cow can produce more than 25 GALLONS (94.6 L) OF MILK a day!

A WEIRD WAY TO
WAKE UP

Knock, knock. Who's there? The knocker-up! An early sort of alarm clock, the knocker-up was a person whose job it was to wake people by tapping on their bedroom window with a long stick. The method may sound annoying, but it worked; the knocker-up would *tap-tap-tap* until the person was up and only then move on to the next house. Their sticks were typically lightweight and sometimes had a metal ball or wire affixed to the tip, to make a louder sound. Customers could make arrangements with the knocker-up ahead of time or simply post on the outside of their home the hour at which they would like to be woken up. Large factories also hired knocker-ups to make sure their employees arrived at work on time. The knocker-ups were usually men, though there was a woman known to use a peashooter to wake up her clients. So … who woke the knocker-ups up?

REAL

HONEST ABE

KNOCKER-UPS APPEARED AROUND THE TIME OF THE INDUSTRIAL REVOLUTION, WHICH STARTED IN BRITAIN IN THE LATE 1700s AND THEN SPREAD TO OTHER PARTS OF THE WORLD. This revolution changed the way people worked, moving them from their homes to factories. Before that, people typically didn't need to start work at a specific time. Traditional bedside alarm clocks weren't in widespread use until the late 1800s.

FUN FACT

In 2015, a woman built an alarm clock that wakes her up by SLAPPING HER IN THE FACE WITH A RUBBER HAND.

PUPPIES PUT ON
POOP PATROL

REAL OR FAKE?

There's a serious problem plaguing the United States' capital, **Washington, D.C.: goose poop.** Piles of poop litter the National Mall, the green stretch of parkland that's home to memorials and monuments and flanked by important buildings such as the Smithsonian museums and U.S. Capitol. Unwilling to allow the fowl to foul the famous lawn, the National Park Service hired another species to solve the dilemma: dogs! Trained border collies, known for their ability to herd sheep, now act as "geese police" on the mall. The dogs don't touch the geese, but they give them a fierce look that sends them flying. The result? There's now less poop clogging the famous reflecting pool and causing problems. The scene may sound funny, but the poop struggle is real: The Park Service says that a single Canada goose can drop two to three pounds (about 1 kg) of poop a day!

CITATION

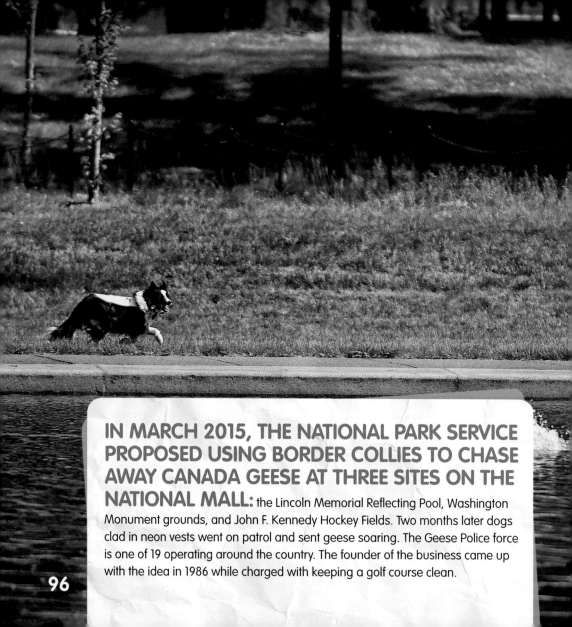

IN MARCH 2015, THE NATIONAL PARK SERVICE PROPOSED USING BORDER COLLIES TO CHASE AWAY CANADA GEESE AT THREE SITES ON THE NATIONAL MALL: the Lincoln Memorial Reflecting Pool, Washington Monument grounds, and John F. Kennedy Hockey Fields. Two months later dogs clad in neon vests went on patrol and sent geese soaring. The Geese Police force is one of 19 operating around the country. The founder of the business came up with the idea in 1986 while charged with keeping a golf course clean.

HONEST ABE

REAL

FUN FACT

CANADA GEESE are very protective of their young. They will charge an animal as big as an elk!

IDENTIFY THE LIE!

For each question group below, two statements are TRUE, and one is FALSE. Can you put your finger on the fib?

1

A. The smallest book in the world can be read only with a magnifying glass.

B. There is a world's largest pig hair ball, and it resides in a museum outside Mount Angel, Oregon.

C. A horologist is a clock expert.

2

A. The paint on some public walls in San Francisco, California, makes pee splash back on offenders.

B. On their journey from lakes, rivers, and streams to the sea, young salmon swim sideways.

C. A Florida woman owns a six-foot (2-m) pet gator, named Rambo, who rides a motorcycle.

ANSWERS: 1. A: Fake! The tiniest book ever, *Teeny Ted from Turnip Town*, is too small to be read even with a magnifying glass! You need a scanning electron microscope, which magnifies an image up to 30,000 times! 2. B: Fake! Young salmon travel from their freshwater birthplace to the sea swimming backward, not sideways. The fish travel tail-first because they're following the flow of the water to the ocean. This way, they don't have to expend energy swimming.

TISSUES:
NOT FOR NOSES!

Have you been using tissue paper to blow your nose? If so, you're blowing it: The fine print on the bottom of a box of tissues states, "This product is not intended for use on or in the nose. Instead it should be used for dabbing the corners of the mouth or the eyes. Use of this product near the nose could be harmful to your health." Though tissues and noses go together like cotton swabs and ears, tissues should stay away from your schnoz. The misuse started in the early 1970s, when an episode of a popular TV series showed the sick family using tissues for their stuffy and runny noses, and tissue sales skyrocketed! So why the worry over using tissues on your nose? Scientists say the scent of the paper products can irritate the delicate lining of the nose and actually cause it to become *more* stuffy or runny!

CAUTION

NOT for NOSES

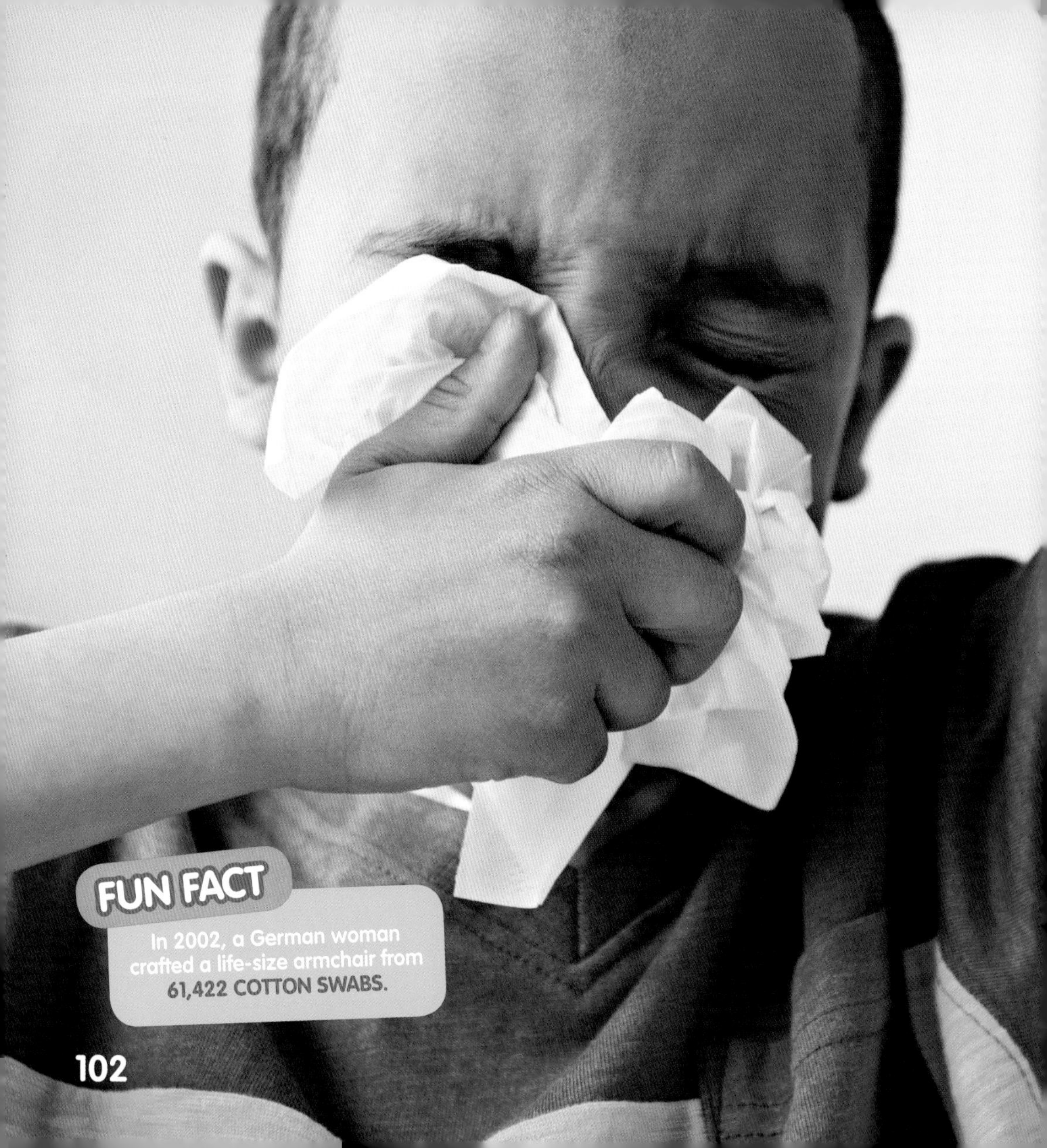

FUN FACT

In 2002, a German woman crafted a life-size armchair from 61,422 COTTON SWABS.

FAKE!

BIG OL' WHOPPER

IT'S FINE TO USE TISSUE PAPER ON YOUR NOSE—SO SNEEZE, WIPE, AND BLOW AWAY. BUT DON'T PUT THAT COTTON SWAB IN YOUR EAR! Those soft little sticks aren't safe for the inside of your ears, according to the makers of a popular brand. A warning on the box reads: "Do not insert swab into ear canal. Entering the ear canal could cause injury. If used to clean ears, stroke swab gently around the outer surface of the ear only."

A TAX
ON BEARDS

REAL OR FAKE?

Beards and mustaches are more popular than ever, with events drawing thousands from around the world each year to celebrate chin whiskers. But there have been multiple times throughout history when facial hair fell out of favor and people literally paid a price for letting it grow. As far back as the 1500s, kings ordered anyone with a beard to pay a tax, or portion of money, to the government. The wealthier someone was, the more money they had to pay the government. This meant that sporting a beard could be a status symbol: Someone was so rich they could afford not to shave. In the 1700s, Russia's Peter the Great gave beard taxpayers coins that proved they had paid. Before that, though, he was so anti-beard that he ordered policemen to shave offenders on sight!

REAL

HONEST
ABE

PEOPLE HAVE BEEN FINED FOR THEIR FACIAL HAIR FOR HUNDREDS OF YEARS. It may sound odd, but it makes sense when you think of it as a clever way for governments to collect more money from their citizens. Other silly things have also been taxed throughout history, including everything from wallpaper to blueberries.

HOVERBOARDS
ARE HERE!

REAL OR FAKE?

In March 2014, a video making a shocking announcement was released online: Hoverboards, the futuristic floating devices depicted in a popular movie, are finally here! Called the HUVr Board, it looks like a skateboard sans wheels and enables users to hover in the air. In the video, skateboard pro Tony Hawk attends a demonstration for the new gadget in Los Angeles. There he hops onto a HUVr and floats through the air, exclaiming, "I can't believe how well it works!" To show how easy it is to ride a HUVr, the company also asked a few famous non-skateboarders to try it out, including musician Moby and pro football player Terrell Owens. The video shows them flying through the air with ease. The millions of people who watched the video clamored to figure out where to buy one!

FAKE!

LITTLE
WHITE LIE

There is a real product called a hoverboard but it doesn't actually float in the air like the fictional HUVr. Instead the hoverboard looks like A FIGURE-8-SHAPED SKATEBOARD WITH A WHEEL AT EACH END.

AN ONLINE COMEDY SITE LATER ADMITTED THEY WERE BEHIND THE FAKE VIDEO, WHICH PULLED OUT ALL THE STOPS, SUCH AS SPECIAL EFFECTS AND CELEBRITY CAMEOS, TO SEEM REAL. The fake website for the company, HUVr Tech, seemed professional, even including a photo of the team of creators with a description of them as "materials science, electricity & magnetism experts who've solved an important part of one of science's mysteries: the key to antigravity."

REAL OR FAKE?

INVENTIONS

They say necessity is the mother of invention, but it's hard to believe people saw a need for these crazy creations! Check out the products below and decide which of these wild wares are REAL, and which are just the figment of a WILD imagination.

1 FLIP-FLOPS THAT FEEL LIKE YOU'RE WALKING ON GRASS

2 DEVICE THAT DE-KERNELS CORN

3 PLASTIC PLANT HEADWEAR

4 NOSE DEVICE THAT MAKES SNORES SOUND LIKE PURRS

5 TV REMOTE THAT LOOKS AND ACTS LIKE A MAGIC WAND

6 EYE CONTACTS THAT SHOOT LASER BEAMS

SELFIE TOASTER **7**

MINI-HAMMOCK FOR FEET **8**

ANSWERS: 1. Real; 2. Real; 3. Real; 4. Fake; 5. Real; 6. Real; 7. Fake; 8. Real

POOP CAUSES
BIG OOPS!

Answering the call of nature while out in nature seems like a perfectly, well, natural thing to do. But one man on a bike ride near Boise, Idaho, U.S.A., showed how an outdoors bathroom break can go horribly awry. He had been mountain biking in the foothills around the city and stopped to go number two in a small valley. In an effort to clean up the mess, he lit his used toilet paper on fire … and, accidentally, 73 acres (29.5 ha) of forest! An ember from the toilet paper flames set the surrounding grass—which was very dry—on fire, and the blaze spread from there. Firefighters manning trucks, bulldozers, and helicopters spent six hours putting out the flames. Afterward, the sheepish man stepped forward to claim responsibility and apologize for starting a fire. He said all he had wanted to do was avoid littering!

REAL

HONEST
ABE

THIS EMBARRASSING ACCIDENT HAPPENED IN SUMMER 2015.

The man, whose name was not released to the public, was given a citation. Police were still deciding whether to charge him with a crime and make him pay for the cost—thousands of dollars—of his poop oops. The national news coverage of the story helped spread the word that you should never burn toilet paper. Instead you should bury it or carry it out!

FUN FACT

In the middle ages, before toilet paper was invented, people wiped with a "GOMPF STICK": a sponge stuck on the end of a stick.

MAN BECOMES
SCIENCE PROJECT

REAL OR FAKE?

Do you have a favorite animal? Yuri Lukovich does. It's a badger. And his love for the animal goes beyond anyone else's: Lukovich has asked scientists to give him badger genes in an effort to make him part man, part animal. It sounds bonkers, but recent advances in genetics could make the Moscow, Russia, millionaire's dream come true. Starting in 2017, he'll receive weekly and then daily injections of badger DNA. Lukovich is working closely with a team of handpicked scientists to choose which genes are in and which are out. For example, Lukovich would like to be able to dig as a badger does, but not have the animal's musky smell. Lukovich thinks the transformation will be awesome. But not everyone agrees. An international team of scientists signed a petition to try to stop the experiment, calling it "dangerous." Two notable signatures on the petition: his parents. As his father said, "We didn't raise him to be a badger. We raised him to be a human."

FAKE!

LITTLE WHITE LIE

THERE IS NO MILLIONAIRE NAMED YURI LUKOVICH, AND NO SCIENCE EXPERIMENT UNDERWAY TO CREATE A HUMAN-ANIMAL HYBRID, LIKE AN X-MEN CHARACTER. But one man did take his love of badgers to the extreme. In 2016's *Being a Beast: Adventures Across the Species Divide,* author Charles Foster lived as a badger in the mountains of Wales, United Kingdom. He became nocturnal, dug and slept in a dirt hole, and ate live earthworms.

APE FOOLS
ART CRITICS

REAL OR FAKE?

A Swedish journalist wanted to put art critics to the test: Could they tell whether an ape or a person had painted a picture? So he convinced the handler of Peter, a four-year-old West African chimpanzee at the Borås zoo, to give his charge some paintbrushes, colors, and canvases and see what the chimp could create. Peter painted 10 pictures, all of which looked like scribbles. He also painted his handler and the floor, and ate several tubes of blue paint along with some bananas. The paintings were then hung in a gallery under the name "Pierre Brassau." The reviews were mostly positive. One critic said, "Pierre Brassau paints with powerful strokes, but also with clear determination ... Pierre is an artist who performs with the delicacy of a ballet dancer." It wasn't until afterward that the reviewers were told that Pierre wasn't a person—he was an ape!

REAL

HONEST
ABE

IN 1964, A JOURNALIST AT A SWEDISH
NEWSPAPER PULLED THIS PRANK ON
ART CRITICS AT OTHER NEWSPAPERS.
Not all of the critics were fooled, though. One reviewer wrote that he
wasn't impressed with Pierre's painting, and said, "Only an ape could
have done this." How right he was!

125

DOGS SNEEZE
IN REVERSE

REAL OR FAKE?

Dogs can walk backward. But did you know they can sneeze backward, too? This isn't just a fancy trick to get a treat. A reverse sneeze, as veterinarians call it, is a way for dogs to clear the upper part of their nasal passages. Instead of blowing air out of their noses—like in a sneeze—they forcefully sniff air into their noses. They do this rapidly and repeatedly, creating a loud, weird noise. If you've never seen a reverse sneeze, the sight and sound of one may be worrisome. But it can be a totally normal way for the dog to clear irritants from the back of its nose. And it usually lasts less than a minute. So can people perform backward sneezes? You can try, but it might not work the same way it does in dogs. And people (and your pup) may look at you funny.

HONEST ABE

REAL

A REVERSE SNEEZE IS ONE MORE AMAZING FEAT THAT DOGS CAN DO. Veterinarians regularly see pups whose owners bring them in because they saw the sneeze and freaked out. Often it's normal, although occasionally it's not. For example, if your dog seems to be sneezing—backward *or forward*—a lot, it's good to get it checked out.

REAL OR FAKE?

ANIMAL SNEEZES

Humans aren't the only animals that get the sniffles. Can you guess which of the following facts are TRUE, and which are MADE UP?

1 Marine iguanas squirt salt from their noses during a sneeze.

2 Baboons are the only primates that don't sneeze.

3 Nobody knows if insects are able to sneeze.

130

4 Elephants sneeze through their mouths instead of their trunks—they're too long!

5 Fish sneeze in order to clear their gills.

6 Cats sneeze only during the day, never at night.

7 The spray from a woodpecker's sneeze is so strong that it can punch a tiny hole in a tree.

ANSWERS: 1. True; 2. False; 3. True; 4. False; 5. True; 6. False; 7. False

BABYSITTERS FOR ROCKS

REAL OR FAKE?

Pet rocks are weird. They don't breathe, they don't bite, and they don't go to the bathroom. They're simply rocks that people call pets. But what's weirder: Pet-rock owners have started hiring babysitters to watch over their precious stones! What in the world does a pet-rock babysitter do? One website promises to "dust your pet rock, sing softly to it, pet it, and move it around the house for a change of scenery." The service is totally silly, but that hasn't stopped it from taking off in Japan and China. (And websites offering the service in the United States and Canada are coming online, too.) One in-demand pet-rock babysitter explains: "The owners know their rocks aren't real pets, but that doesn't matter. They like their things, alive or not, well cared for." So how much does a rock-sitter cost? Some companies charge as much as $75 an hour!

FAKE!

BIG OL' WHOPPER

PET ROCKS ARE REAL: MORE THAN A MILLION WERE SOLD FOR $3.95 EACH AFTER THEY FIRST HIT STORES IN 1975. But babysitters for them aren't. As the Pet Rock website points out, these pets don't need to be fed or walked, are "pre-trained to 'sit' and 'stay' and best of all … will never run away!" You can still buy a pet rock today, for under $20!

FUN FACT

A PET ROCK is sold in a box with air holes (so it can breathe).

135

MILLION-DOLLAR MISTAKE

What's worse than tripping and punching a hole in a priceless piece of art? A video of the accident going viral and people around the world seeing it! A 12-year-old boy in Taipei, Taiwan, was perusing pricey paintings in a gallery when he suddenly stumbled, fell into a rope intended to protect the art, and broke his fall by putting his hand through a 17th-century painting. The video shows he was clearly stunned after the accident. He straightens himself up, and then stares at the painting as a crowd of people gathers around him. The punched painting—"Flowers," a still life that depicts blossoms in a vase—is the work of Italian artist Paolo Porpora and is valued at $1.5 million. Luckily, the artwork was insured, so the boy and his family weren't asked to pay for repairs. Though experts can restore the painting, it will never be the same.

HONEST
ABE

REAL

THIS NIGHTMARISH BLUNDER HAPPENED IN AUGUST 2015. The boy who tripped isn't alone, though, when it comes to arty accidents. A man stumbled on his shoelace and smashed three 300-plus-year-old Chinese vases in Cambridge, England, U.K., in 2006. And in 2010 a woman in New York City fell into a Picasso painting, putting a six-inch (15-cm) tear in it.

RUGBY PLAYER
TURNS TO TICKLING

REAL OR FAKE?

In 2014, the rough sport of rugby got a little gentler when famed New Zealand All Blacks player Ethan Femwaller found a funny way to distract his opponents: by tickling them! Rugby is known for its full-body contact that regularly leaves players banged up. Femwaller turned to tickling, he explained, because it's kinder but still causes players to lose their coordination (and hopefully the ball they're holding). The first time he let loose his fingers on an opponent, the confused player asked that Femwaller be penalized. But when the referee looked at the rule book, he saw no mention of tickling. So Femwaller kept at it. Eventually a group of players from 12 other teams demanded that the rules be revised. Rugby officials agreed, but a stubborn Femwaller refused to stop tickling. So he was banned from all future games!

FAKE!

LITTLE
WHITE LIE

WHILE THE NEW ZEALAND ALL BLACKS ARE A REAL TEAM, THERE IS NO PLAYER NAMED ETHAN FEMWALLER, AND NO ONE HAS BEEN BANNED FROM THE SPORT FOR TICKLING (LET ALONE KNOWN FOR IT). Uruguayan soccer player Luis Suárez made international news in 2014, though, after he bit an opponent during a World Cup game. It wasn't even his first time—he'd bitten other players twice before! For his World Cup offense, he was fined $94,000 and banned from games for four months.

143

WEIRD MOMENTS IN
SPORTS

REAL OR FAKE?

Can you tell which of the following outrageous sports stories are REAL and which are MADE UP? Game on!

1. During a World Cup game, someone threw a cantaloupe onto the soccer field and some of the players mistook it for the ball.

2. An Olympic swimmer wore a snorkel and mask while competing in the 200-meter freestyle.

3. A college football coach got caught on camera picking his nose and eating a booger during a nationally televised game.

4. A horse confused the judges at an international equestrian event when it completed its program but did so backward.

5. During an Italian soccer match, a player head-butted the bench and received a red card.

6. A boxer bit off part of his opponent's ear during a championship bout.

7. Someone switched one of the route signs for the Tour de France and half the cyclists got lost.

ROCK-HARD
HOTEL

REAL OR FAKE?

You've probably heard the saying "sleep like a rock," which means to sleep well. But have you ever heard of actually sleeping on a rock? In Sydney, Australia, the latest trend is hotels with beds that are simply slabs of stone. No mattress, no pillows. But comforters and sheets are provided, in case you get chilly (or stone-cold). Supposedly the stone supports the spine just fine, and is, in fact, better than something softer, such as a traditional mattress. Monks in Australia's Yarra Valley who have slept on stone for centuries—and on average live to be older than 100—inspired the hard-rock hotels. After a famous pop star posted on social media about her great night of sleep in one of the rooms, bookings increased exponentially. There's now a six-month waiting list to check in to any of the hotels!

FAKE!

LITTLE
WHITE LIE

FUN FACT

In ancient Egypt, beds
slanted downward and
had a footboard at the
bottom to STOP SLEEPERS
FROM SLIDING OFF.

THOUGH THIS TREND IS MADE UP, THERE ARE ROOMS THAT OFFER A SOMEWHAT SIMILAR EXPERIENCE IN SWEDEN'S ICEHOTEL. Made of ice and snow, it was first sculpted in 1989 and its below-freezing rooms feature bed frames (and walls, ceilings, and so on) carved from ice. The whole hotel must be re-created each year—it melts in the spring!

KID KING IS A
ROYAL PAIN

REAL OR FAKE?

In the middle of the South Pacific Ocean lives a kid who doesn't have to follow any rules, plus he gets to make them up for everyone else! Meet King Crimson Crowder IV, ruler of the remote island country of Yandon. He ascended to the throne at age 6, after his older sister abdicated (a fancy word for left) to race cars. Immediately, KCC (as he's called by the citizens of Yandon, though never to his face) assumed control of the country and began to make astonishing changes. First, he filled the palace swimming pool with chocolate syrup. Next, he banned eggplants—his least favorite food—from the country. Then he announced school was optional for all children over the age of 10! Ever since, children have championed the king while adults fear him. It's rumored that anyone who questions KCC's authority is immediately ordered off the island!

FAKE!

LITTLE
WHITE LIE

FUN FACT

No kid could ever be in charge of the United States of America: The president must be at least **35 YEARS OLD.**

THERE IS NO KING CRIMSON CROWDER IV. (A BUMMER TO KIDS, BUT A RELIEF TO ADULTS.) Nor is there a country named Yandon. But there have been many young rulers of numerous countries throughout history. Perhaps the most famous is King Tutankhamun, aka King Tut, who assumed the throne of ancient Egypt at age 9, more than 3,000 years ago.

153

JUSTICE AT YOUR
FINGERTIPS

REAL OR FAKE?

Did you know that even identical twins have different finger-prints? That's why it's the only reliable way to tell people apart, as a crazy case of near mistaken identity in 1903 showed. That year a convicted criminal named Will West was taken to a prison in Leavenworth, Kansas, U.S.A. The clerk who checked in West thought he recognized him and asked if he'd been there before. West replied that he hadn't, but the clerk thought for sure he had seen him. When the clerk checked the prison's records he found a file for a William West, who looked identical to Will West—but was already inside the prison, serving a life sentence! Incredibly, the two men had nearly identical faces and names (and may have been twins, unbeknownst to them). Their fingerprints, taken shortly thereafter, clearly showed, though, that they were two different people. News of the case spread across the country and with it the practice of regularly fingerprinting criminals.

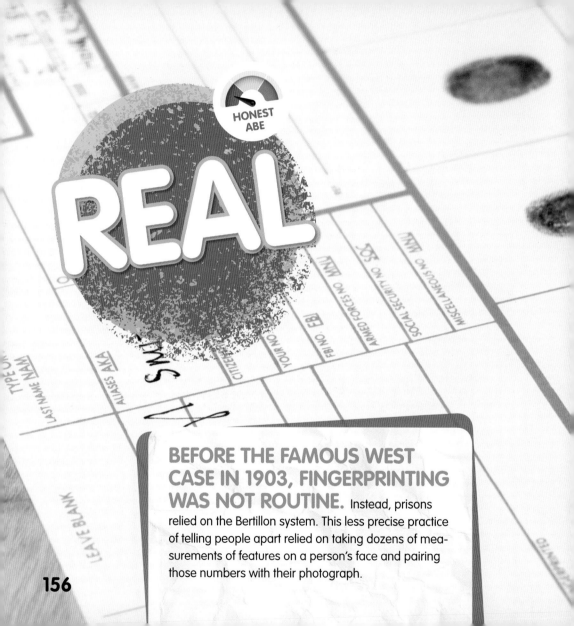

HONEST ABE

REAL

BEFORE THE FAMOUS WEST CASE IN 1903, FINGERPRINTING WAS NOT ROUTINE. Instead, prisons relied on the Bertillon system. This less precise practice of telling people apart relied on taking dozens of measurements of features on a person's face and pairing those numbers with their photograph.

FUN FACT

According to FBI rules, if someone has an EXTRA FINGER, prints are recorded for only their thumb and the next four fingers.

SPOT THE FAKE!

Do you have the eye of a spy? See if you can tell which of these photos are REAL, and which are really FAKE!

1

A girl in North Carolina, U.S.A., trained her pet turtle to catch—but it can't throw!

2

This rubber ducky was too big for the bath, so instead it bobbed in a Hong Kong harbor.

1

A green tree frog looks like it has the head of a budwing mantis, but really it's about to devour its next meal.

2

A superstrong weaver ant balances a hapless centipede.

SCRABBLE STAR'S
WACKY WIN

To play the board game Scrabble well, you need to be a whiz with words. But you don't necessarily need to know what those words mean—even when it comes to winning a world championship game. In 2015, a New Zealand man who doesn't speak a lick of French won the French-language world Scrabble competition! Nigel Richards bested his French-speaking competitors by memorizing the French Scrabble dictionary, which contains every French word between two and 10 letters long. And he did so in only nine weeks! Though he doesn't know what the French words mean, he remembers them by their letter sequences. After he was declared the winner at the competition, held in Louvain-la-Neuve, Belgium, the amazed, mostly French-speaking audience gave him a standing ovation. Richards, who speaks only English fluently, thanked the crowd through a translator.

I DON'T SPEAK FRENCH

REAL

HONEST
ABE

NIGEL RICHARDS TOOK HOME THE TITLE AT THE FRENCH-SPEAKING WORLD SCRABBLE CHAMPIONSHIP DESPITE NOT KNOWING THE LANGUAGE! It's not the first time he's won one of the international board game competitions. He's also won the English-speaking world Scrabble championship three times. But it's the first time anyone has ever taken home the title without understanding the language.

IDENTIFY THE LIE!

For each question group below, two statements are TRUE, and one is FALSE. Can you put your finger on the fib?

1

A. Famous basketball player Shaquille O'Neal also has a degree in dentistry.

B. *Pareidolia* is the word for when people see shapes such as a person's face on a piece of toast.

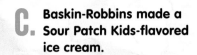

C. Baskin-Robbins made a Sour Patch Kids-flavored ice cream.

2

A. Ancient peoples used glow-in-the-dark mushrooms as flashlights.

B. Astronauts are up to two inches (5 cm) taller while in space.

C. A giraffe at the San Diego Zoo learned how to use a crutch for three months after it broke its leg.

ANSWERS: 1. A: Fake! Shaquille O'Neal isn't a dentist, but he does have a Ph.D.! He received his doctorate in education from Barry University in 2012. O'Neal, who stands 7 feet 1 inch tall, reportedly wore a size XXXL graduation gown. 2. C: Fake! The giraffe story is just a tall tale. But staff at the Seattle Aquarium did train a sea otter how to use an inhaler for her asthma! Mishka is the first sea otter to be diagnosed with the disease. Her medication is the same one given to people with asthma!

MAN SETS FIRE
OVER SPIDER

REAL OR FAKE?

Some ideas seem good at the time. Some ideas seem good, well, never. A Seattle, Washington, U.S.A., man terrified of spiders accidentally set his house on fire and nearly burned it down after using a homemade blowtorch to try to get rid of an eight-legged critter. The blaze began in the laundry room at night, when after spying the spider, in a fit of fear and desperation, the man used a lighter and a can of spray paint to create a fireball. (It can only be assumed that he did not have a fear of fire.) It's unknown whether he scorched the spider, but what did happen: The fire spread to the attic and firefighters were called to the scene. They managed to put out the flames, but the home was so damaged the man had to move out. The cost of his catastrophe: $60,000!

REAL

HONEST
ABE

FUN FACT

ARACHNOPHOBIA is the word for an intense fear of spiders. An intense fear of fire is called pyrophobia.

DON'T TRY THIS AT HOME!

IN 2014, ONE MAN SWAPPED A LITTLE PROBLEM FOR A REALLY BIG ONE WHEN HE SPOTTED A SPIDER TRYING TO CRAWL INTO HIS HOME'S WALL AND ATTEMPTED TO SET THE INTRUDER ON FIRE. His mistake was reported around the world. But perhaps the worst part was that he was renting the house—he wasn't even its owner!

171

WOLF WANDERS
OLYMPIC DORM

REAL OR FAKE?

Athletes competing in the 2014 Winter Olympics in Sochi, Russia, saw some strange sights for sure. But the biggest surprise came for one U.S. athlete who saw a shocking scene right in her hotel: a wolf! Luger Kate Hansen posted a shocking video of what appeared to be a wolf wandering outside her room to her social media accounts, exclaiming, "Wolf in my hall?!?" The scary sighting soon went viral, with the popular hashtags #SochiProblems and #SochiFail. Was it a wild wolf that had somehow found its way inside? Someone's pet? A wolflike stray dog? An animal athlete? Whatever it was, no one saw it again, and, most importantly, no one got hurt!

FUN FACT

Some of the athletes competing in the 2014 Winter Olympics adopted and brought home **STRAY DOGS FROM THE STREETS OF SOCHI.**

FAKE!

BIG OL' WHOPPER

THE WOLF IN THE HALLWAY WAS A PRANK PULLED BY KATE HANSEN AND U.S. TALK SHOW HOST JIMMY KIMMEL.

The host had a replica of an Olympic Village dorm built and hired a wolf for the silly short video, filmed in America. A few days after it aired online, Kimmel and Hansen admitted it was fake. Most people found it funny, including Olympic officials … sort of. An International Olympic Committee spokesman said, "It made me kind of laugh as an individual, not as an IOC spokesman."

ONE MIGHTY
MUSHROOM

REAL OR FAKE?

What's bigger than a blue whale, more enormous than an elephant, and weighs far more than any dinosaur ever did? The answer may surprise you: a humongous fungus that lives beneath the forest floor in eastern Oregon! It's the world's largest organism, spanning about 2,200 acres (890 ha)—or 1,665 football fields! And it weighs as much as 35,000 tons (31,750 t). What's more: This behemoth is also a killer. Scientists found out about the fungus when investigating the death of more than a hundred trees in the Oregon forest. After digging around, they identified a so-called honey mushroom as the culprit. When scientists examined the fungus cells found on various trees—some miles apart from each other—they were shocked to find that they belonged to a single organism, the humongous fungus!

REAL

HONEST ABE

THE HUMONGOUS FUNGUS LIVES!

The discovery of this *Armillaria ostoyae* was big news when it was announced in 2000. And it isn't just the largest living organism. It's also very old: about 2,400 years, scientists estimate, and it could even be three times older than that.

FUN FACT

Humans are more closely related to MUSHROOMS than to plants.

BIG APPLE BRIDGE
FOR SALE

In the late 1800s and early 1900s, anyone off the street could buy New York City's iconic Brooklyn Bridge and erect their own tolls at the ends to collect cash from travelers. You just had to find the current owner, which wasn't hard thanks to the "Bridge for Sale" signs. And, of course, you had to have enough money to buy the bridge, which spans the East River and connects the boroughs, or neighborhoods, of Manhattan and Brooklyn. Because it was so easy to buy, its ownership changed hands many times, usually among immigrants who recently arrived in the Big Apple. The newcomers were delighted to discover that America truly was the land of opportunity, and even something as big and beautiful as the bridge could be bought. It sold for anywhere between $200 and $1,000. Once, only half the bridge was sold, for $250, when an interested customer didn't have enough cash to buy the whole thing!

FUN FACT

When the Brooklyn Bridge opened in 1883, IT WAS THE LONGEST SUSPENSION BRIDGE IN THE WORLD. Its long central span stretches 1,595 feet (486 m).

FAKE!

BIG OL' WHOPPER

BUYING THE BROOKLYN BRIDGE IS AN INFAMOUS SCAM FROM THE 19TH AND 20TH CENTURIES. Con artists with forged documents kept an eye on police routes and when they weren't around set up the "Bridge for Sale" signs. They preyed on immigrants, who were new to America and didn't yet know the laws or speak the language well. Buyers often didn't know they'd been duped until they tried to put up tolls and were forced off by police!

CRUDE
LUXURY SPA

REAL OR FAKE?

The town of Naftalan, Azerbaijan, is world-famous for its special spa baths, despite the fact that they are downright crude—crude oil, that is. Bathtubs filled with brown-black oil sucked up from the earth draw thousands of people to this vacation spot between the Black and Caspian Seas. People claim that sitting in the oil can help cure dozens of diseases. Doctors aren't so sure. Still, plenty of people pay to soak in a tub of oil for just 10 minutes. That's far less time than it takes for a spa employee to wipe and wash off all the oil afterward (it's as messy as you would imagine). If the idea of bathing in oil doesn't disgust you, there's also this to consider: The oil you sit in isn't only for you—it's reused from bather to bather!

REAL

HONEST ABE

FOR DECADES PEOPLE HAVE FLOCKED TO NAFTALAN TO TAKE A NICE, RELAXING BATH IN CRUDE OIL. That's the same stuff used to make gasoline! It sounds crazy, but some people swear by the spa's supposed powers. The town even boasts a museum full of crutches said to be left behind by bathers whose problems were cured.

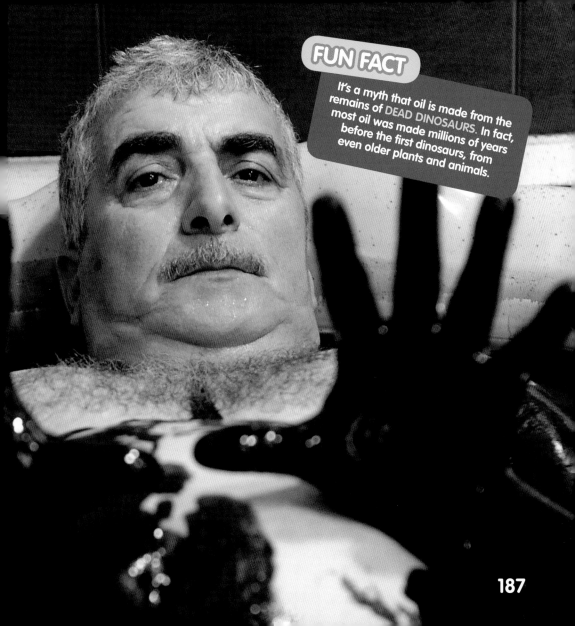

FUN FACT

It's a myth that oil is made from the remains of DEAD DINOSAURS. In fact, most oil was made millions of years before the first dinosaurs, from even older plants and animals.

FAKE CROWDS AND FANS FOR HIRE

REAL OR FAKE?

The next time you see a crowd of fans, think twice. They may be fake. A business called Crowds on Demand hires people to pose as fans and paparazzi as a way to make people feel special. Based in Beverly Hills, California, the business offers services such as Celebrity Shopping Experience and Celebrity Airport Greeting. For a fee, actors will swarm around you and pose as your biggest fans—chanting your name, begging for an autograph, and snapping pics—while you wander expensive stores, eat at the finest restaurants, or simply just arrive at the airport. Plenty of people hire a crowd to create a buzz around themselves, but the company's website suggests using their services to make loved ones, co-workers, and clients feel special, too. Don't live in California? No problem: Crowds can be hired in big cities from Seattle, Washington, to Miami, Florida.

HONEST ABE

REAL

CROWDS ON DEMAND HAS BEEN MAKING PEOPLE FEEL SPECIAL SINCE 2012. The company relies on more than 500 actors across the country to create the crowds. They're also available for hire for protests and political events.

FUN FACT

In 2014, a crowd of football fans cheering on the Kansas City Chiefs created the LOUDEST ROAR EVER in a sports stadium: 142.2 decibels, about as loud as a jet engine during takeoff.

TRAIN AT THE
TOP OF THE WORLD

REAL OR FAKE?

Siberia and northern Alaska, U.S.A., are some of the most sparsely populated, frigid places on Earth. But they were once home to one of the most impressive transportation feats ever: A 155-mile (250-km)-long railroad bridge across the Bering Strait that allowed Asia and North America to exchange goods. Built by Russian engineers over 53 years, the Top of the World Railway was finally completed in 1867. It ferried countless metals, wood products, furs, and art between the two continents. A hardy but small population of workers was stationed at both ends of the railway to keep things running and assist in transporting the goods from trains to horses and ships. Sadly, it had been operating for only seven years when a magnitude 8 earthquake in the North Pacific shook the bridge from its foundation and sent it toppling into the sea. To this day, a train full of precious goods sits on the bottom of the sea, forever out of reach.

FUN FACT

In 2015, the head of Russian Railways proposed building an UNDERWATER TUNNEL ACROSS THE BERING STRAIT that could be used by both high-speed trains and cars!

A 155-MILE (250-KM)-LONG BRIDGE WOULD HAVE BEEN SOME FEAT, ESPECIALLY ONE BUILT BACK IN THE 1800s AND IN A FROZEN LANDSCAPE. The longest bridge in the world is only 102 miles (164 km) long (still impressive!) and was built in China in 2011. And only some 60 miles (96 km) separate Russia from Alaska at the Bering Strait. But tens of thousands of years ago, when sea levels were lower, a massive land bridge sat where the strait is today, connecting the two continents.

FAKE!

BIG OL' WHOPPER

SPOT THE FAKE!

Do you have the eye of a spy? See if you can tell which of these photos are REAL and which are really FAKE!

1

Up close, this man's teeny-tiny museum looks like the real thing.

This giraffe's colorful coat was the envy of a black-and-white zebra.

2

Look out below! Unidentified flying objects (UFOs) hover just outside of Los Angeles, California.

2

This funny photo of a weasel riding a woodpecker became an Internet sensation in 2015.

1

A zonkey, a cross between a zebra and a donkey

2

A cloud question mark

INDEX

Illustrations are indicated by **boldface**.

CREDITS